The Massachusetts Bay Color
Cc

By Charles River Editors

The Flag of the Colony

About Charles River Editors

Charles River Editors provides superior editing and original writing services across the digital publishing industry, with the expertise to create digital content for publishers across a vast range of subject matter. In addition to providing original digital content for third party publishers, we also republish civilization's greatest literary works, bringing them to new generations of readers via ebooks.

Sign up here to receive updates about free books as we publish them, and visit Our Kindle Author Page to browse today's free promotions and our most recently published Kindle titles.

The Massachusetts Bay Colony: The History and Legacy of the Settlement of Colonial New England

About Charles River Editors

Chapter 1: The Massachusetts Bay Company

Chapter 2: Starting a Settlement

Chapter 3: John Winthrop

Chapter 4: The Great Migration

Chapter 5: Economy

Chapter 6: Family Life

Chapter 7: Indian Relations

Chapter 8: Memoir of Roger Clap

Chapter 9: Dealing with Dissent

Chapter 10: Anne Hutchinson

Chapter 10: Roger Williams

Chapter 11: The End of Massachusetts Bay

Online Resources

Bibliography

Chapter 1: The Massachusetts Bay Company

The Colony's Seal

The first successful American colony in North America was settled in 1607 at Jamestown, Virginia. Though the Virginian colonists had difficulty in the beginning, by the late 1620s the Chesapeake area was thriving, having become a haven for those seeking economic opportunity in the new world.[1] Pressures in England were growing as King Charles I was on the throne. Though Charles I himself was an Anglican, many suspected him of Catholic sympathies, a suspicion not alleviated by Charles I marriage to a French Catholic princess. Many Protestants had a growing desire to practice their faith and conduct their lives away from the mother country, and sought refuge in a destination called New England. The land chosen by this group, who "could pay their own way across the Atlantic"[2] in contrast to the poorer settlers of the Chesapeake region was "colder, less abundant, but far healthier"[3] than Virginia. Alan Taylor sees this decision as one in "classic Puritan fashion", citing one settler's view: "If men desire to

---

[1] Alan Taylor. *American Colonies*. New York: Viking, 2001. 159.
[2] Ibid.
[3] Ibid.

have a people degenerate speedily, and to corrupt their minds and bodies too...let them seek a rich soil, that beings in much with little labor; but if they desire that Piety and Godliness should prosper...let them choose a Country such as [New England] which yields sufficiency with hard labor and industry."[4] The Puritans who came to America were, therefore, primed for hard work, discipline and the independent life, unlike their English counterparts who "preferred Anglicanism and the traditional culture characterized by church ales, Sunday diversions, ceremonial services, inclusive churches, and deference to the monarch."[5] Though James I had seen the connection between the Puritans and challenge to the monarchy, an uneasy peace existed between the two groups until Charles I came to the throne, dissolving Parliament and steering the direction of the English government back toward absolutism.[6]

Charles I of England

During Charles I's reign, William Laud was named the Archbishop of Canterbury. Laud brought with him practices that seemed, to many Puritans, suspiciously Catholic. Laud's actions included the moving of the communion table to a fenced area in the church. This was especially concerning to Puritans because the move implied that the elements of communion were

---

[4] Ibid.
[5] Ibid., 162.
[6] Ibid., 164.

somehow mystical, that they contained the actual body and blood of Christ, a Catholic doctrine known as transubstantiation. Under Laud, the persecution of the Puritans also began in earnest, with men who critiqued the doctrine or moral life of notables locked in the Tower of London. Many of these men were educated attorneys and writers, and were considered to be persons of influence who must be stopped.[7]

Archbishop William Laud

The men of the New England Company decided that the time had come to remove themselves from England, and to pursue their lives in the Americas. The Dorchester Company was founded by a group of investors with an interest in settlement in the New World. This settlement would be a for-profit venture, but would have as its two main causes the spreading of the Gospel to the Indian population and the stop of the spread of Roman Catholicism in the American colonies. John White, the company's leader, also wanted to compete with the separatists who had begun the Plymouth colony in 1620. Cape Ann, a promontory very near to Cape Cod was established by the Dorchester Company as an early settlement. The fishing was excellent, but Cape Ann proved unable to provide the farm goods needed to sustain the Puritan settlers who came to the

---

[7] Ted Morgan. *Wilderness at Dawn: The Settling of the North American Continent.* New York: Simon and Schuster, 1993. 166.

New World.[8] The Dorchester Company was dissolved, but investors seeking to salvage its aims formed the New England Company or Massachusetts Bay Company and secured a charter just before King Charles I dissolved the Parliament in 1629.

By 1629, Winthrop was regarded as a leader by many of the members of the Massachusetts Bay Company and was certainly under consideration for a governing role in the New World. Many, including members of Winthrops' own family, opposed his emigration to the Americas, feeling that he could be better used by God in opposing the Church of England at home, and believing that concerns for his health and safety were paramount.[9] Winthrop eventually devised a list of arguments for both leaving England and settling in New England, called "General Observations." His list of reasons included:

- The desire "to raise a bulwark against the kingdom of Antichrist which the Jesuits labor to raise in all parts of the world" by bringing the Protestant Gospel to America.

- The possibility that churches in Europe were "being brought to desolation it cannot be but that the like judgment is coming upon us;" therefore, the American settlement may be God's place of providence for the "those he meanth to save."

- England's rapidly growing population which described the mother country as one which "groaneth under her inhabitants."
Concern that inflation made it nearly impossible to live at previously standards of living without resorting to ill gain.

- Higher education, including religious education, was corrupt: "The fountains of learning and religion are so corrupted…many children of best wits and fairest hopes are perverted, corrupted, and utterly overthrown by the multitude of evil examples and licentious government of those seminaries."

- In fulfilling the cultural mandate to "till and improve" the land man had been given, men should consider the vastness of land open and available to men in the New World versus the few acres which they might have influence over in England.

- Commitment to the new and growing church in the New World, in order to see the Kingdom of God go forth through his church.

- Changing the currently held views of colonization: If Godly and wealthy men in the old world are willing to "run the hazard with them of a hard and mean condition," it would prove that colonization was about more than amassing wealth and earthly opportunity and encourage others with spiritual motivations to seek the New World.[10]

By 1630 relations between the Puritans and the crown had become so strained that Charles I

[8] Francis J. Bremer, *John Winthrop: America's Forgotten Founding Father* (New York: Oxford University Press, 2003), 152.
[9] Ibid., 155.
[10] Ibid., 157.

was glad to provide a group of wealthy Puritans and their leader, John Winthrop, a charter under the name Massachusetts Bay Company.

Francis Dillon, English author and documentarian, notes that unlike the Pilgrims, the Puritans were "good businessmen" and "obtained a royal charter confirming the grant and a new title: *The Governor and Company of the Massachusetts Bay in New England*."[11] Dillon notes that this action moved the administration of the company itself to America, where it would essentially function as a self-governing colony. Some historical controversy exists on this point. At times, the Puritans have been accused of having absconded to the Americas with the charter, without the knowledge or approval of the King who had granted it and thus operating extra legally. Other historians, however, have sought to defend the Puritans from this charge, citing a document held by the Winthrop family that remained undiscovered until after 1860:

> …a very remarkable paper written by the first Governor, in which he positively and distinctly states that when the charter was in preparation it was sought 'to keep the chief Government in the hands of the Company residing in England, and so this was intended; and with much difficulty we got it abscinded.' This effectually disposes of a plausible charge, and accounts for the absence in the charter of any provision of the place of administration under it.[12]

The company began to take applicants for the voyage, with "desirable" settlers being "first of all Puritan, secondly moneyed, thirdly useful, and the useful category, carpenters, surgeons, sawyers, coopers, and so one, had to be adequate in numbers."[13] Those who dared to join the venture would be carefully vetted since this group of settlers would be no ordinary one.

Chapter 2: Starting a Settlement

The Massachusetts Bay Colony would be marked by two distinctions: a zealous faith and a strong work ethic leading to economic prosperity for its people. The men and women who settled Massachusetts Bay came from a particular religious way of thinking, as a result of the influences of the Protestant Reformation in Europe as well as growing conflict with the Anglican Church. For Puritans, as they were called, the doctrines of the Catholic Church (and to a lesser degree, the Anglican) placed too much emphasis on the individual's desire for salvation and his or her role in it. To the Puritans who were influenced by the doctrines of predestination as set forth by John Calvin, God alone had chosen who would be saved. They hoped for the "'New Birth': a transforming infusion of divine grace that liberated people from profound anxiety over their spiritual worthlessness and eternal fate,"[14] trusting that God's mercy would fall on them. The Puritans grew to criticize the Church of England in areas of practice as well as doctrine.

---

[11] Francis Dillon. *The Pilgrims: Their Journeys and Their World*. New York: Doubleday and Company, 1975.207.
[12] George E. Ellis. *The Puritan Age and Rule in the Colony of the Massachusetts Bay, 1629-1685*. Boston: Houghton Mifflin. 1888.
[13] Ibid., 208.
[14] Ibid., 161.

Most Puritans believed that the official church had retained too much of the aura of Catholicism. They preferred a simpler style of service and faith with less liturgy, less décor, and less formality.

The bridge between the religious and the economic lay in the Puritan regard for and emphasis on the individual. This idea, a legacy of the Reformation, meant in religious terms that a believer could and must approach God personally in prayer and in reading the scriptures. Education was therefore important in this regard and should be provided to both boys and girls. The individual mattered in terms of work and life as well. Calvinist doctrine emphasized God's sovereignty over all the world, and blurred the distinction between the sacred and secular. Hard work, thrift, and accountability for one's actions were therefore markers of the Puritan way of life and thinking. For Puritans "largely under the influence of Scottish and Genevan Calvinism, their theocratic Utopia gave no quarters to religious and civil opposition. It was man's task to know and obey the inexorable Will of God. Every act had a moral aspect, even the most natural acts."[15]

The first successful colonial venture in Massachusetts was Plymouth colony, which had been founded about ten years before the Puritans arrived. It is between these two settlements that the distinction can be made between Pilgrims and Puritans. The Pilgrims, as those in Plymouth came to be known, had some from a different congregation of worshippers and followed particular dynamic leaders to the New World. Thriving at Plymouth became a matter of survival after that leadership died off. Settlers of Plymouth began quarreling over doctrinal issues, worship styles, and discipline within the settlement. About 25 percent of Plymouth's settlers left the colony to return to Europe or move to the colony of Virginia.[16] As a result of the instability, the strict religious structure of Plymouth would become less what the Pilgrims were known for and more descriptive of their Puritan brothers in Massachusetts Bay. As the author of *Mayflower*, Nathaniel Philbrick sees it: "with a clutch of Cambridge-educated divines scripting their every move, the Puritans of Massachusetts Bay developed a more rigorous set of requirements for church membership than had been used at Plymouth…Now, with the arrival of the Puritans in Massachusetts Bay, it was up to others to become the spiritual arbiters of New England."[17]

---

[15] James Ernst. *Roger Williams: New England Firebrand* New York: Macmillan, 1932.88.
[16] Nathaniel Philbrick. *Mayflower: A Story of Courage, Community, and War.* New York: Viking, 2006. 163.
[17] Ibid., 174.

The Embarkation of the Pilgrims

Rather than religious distinctions, which faded relatively quickly after the Puritans arrived in Massachusetts, the distinction between Pilgrims and Puritans came to be made more on the economics and areas of settlement. By 1667, for instance, John Cotton of Massachusetts Bay became the pastor of the Plymouth church. The Pilgrims were known for their infighting and lack of funds, while the Puritans were more "well-to-do and ambitious."[18] Though the melding of the churches came later, some cooperation between Pilgrims and Puritans existed early on. In 1630, just as the Puritans were settling Massachusetts Bay, an infamous Pilgrim settler named John Billington murdered an adversary with whom he had a quarrel. Billington was convicted of the murder by a twelve member jury of fellow Pilgrims, but Pilgrim leaders hesitated to carry out the death penalty, unsure of their judicial authority in the New World.[19] Only after consulting with the newly arrived John Winthrop of Massachusetts Bay, was it decided that Billington must be executed for the murder. It was Winthrop and the Puritans, not the leaders of Plymouth, who carried out the death penalty.[20]

Chapter 3: John Winthrop

John Winthrop and about 400 settlers departed for the new world in 1630. Winthrop sailed on the *Arabella*, leaving his pregnant wife behind to join him in 1631. Both woman and children sailed in the original journey, so the question may be raised as to why Winthrop chose to sail without his wife. A possible explanation lies in the fact that Winthrop had been married twice

[18] Ibid., 175.
[19] Dillon, 204.
[20] Ibid., 177.

already, with both of his wives dying in childbirth. Another 500 settlers came in ships directly behind the *Arabella*, including the *Mayflower*, this time with a group of Bay colonists. Within another year, thousands more had come to the Bay colony, resulting in the largest migration of people coming to the New World at one time, until Penn broke that record in the late 1700s.[21]

John Winthrop

The settlers of what would become the Massachusetts Bay colony arrived in Massachusetts, first making contact with the struggling settlement of Cape Ann. Several sources, including John Winthrop's diary, record the arrival recalling the fine strawberries that the arrivals tasted as soon as they arrived in the summer of 1630.

Winthrop's group of Puritans met their brethren at the Salem church upon arrival, but there was immediate friction between the groups as the Salem Church's minister, Samuel Skelton, refused to serve the leadership of Massachusetts Bay communion, claiming they did not have the

---

[21] John Dickinson, "Chapter V: The Massachusetts Charter and the Bay Colony (1628-1660)," in *Commonwealth History of Massachusetts*, ed. Albert Bushnell Hart, vol. 1 (New York: States History Company, 1927), 100.

proper proof of association from England.[22] After an initial attempt at settling Charlestown, Winthrop's Puritans moved to Boston, and the small size of the peninsula caused the dispersal of the group over nearby settlements that grew into the towns of Watertown and Roxbury.[23]

On the journey, Winthrop composed his famous sermon "A Model of Christian Charity," an explanation and exhortation to the purposes of the new colony. In the sermon, Winthrop laid out the definitions of Christian love (charity), explaining their Biblical origins with specific references to the bearing of one another's burdens in the great experiment on which they were to embark. Winthrop emphasized not only the sameness in the call from God to live to advance his word, just as they had in England, but also the particular calling and work in their new surroundings. From the beginning, Winthrop called the settlers to a higher, covenant purpose and included solemn warnings:

> We are entered into covenant with Him for this work. We have taken out a commission. The Lord hath given us leave to draw our own articles. We have professed to enterprise these and those accounts, upon these and those ends. We have hereupon besought Him of favor and blessing. Now if the Lord shall please to hear us, and bring us in peace to the place we desire, then hath He ratified this covenant and sealed our commission, and will expect a strict performance of the articles contained in it; but if we shall neglect the observation of these articles which are the ends we have propounded, and, dissembling with our God, shall fall to embrace this present world and prosecute our carnal intentions, seeking great things for ourselves and our posterity, the Lord will surely break out in wrath against us, and be revenged of such a people, and make us know the price of the breach of such a covenant.[24]

The covenant concept was familiar both to Winthrop and many of the men in the Massachusetts Bay leadership in both a legal and Biblical sense. As attorneys, they related to the idea of contracts to which both sides were bound, with penalties for non-compliance. Biblically, God had made covenants with Adam, Noah, Moses, Abraham, and David, which now applied to his chosen people, the elect. The sermon made reference to multiple Biblical texts and familiar stories, closing with its most famous passage of exhortation: "For we must consider that we shall be as a city upon a hill. The eyes of all people are upon us. So that if we shall deal falsely with our God in this work we have undertaken, and so cause Him to withdraw His present help from us, we shall be made a story and a by-word through the world."[25] As one historical commentator put it:

> The arrogance of Winthrop and this little settlement of Puritans--the sheer effrontery of this assertion of preeminence--would quickly have been unmasked for its absurdity

---

[22] Morgan, 168.
[23] Ibid., 169.
[24] John Winthrop. "A Model of Christian Charity." 1630. The Winthrop Society.
[25] Ibid.

except for one niggling point, Winthrop turned out to be right. The eyes of much of the world have been upon the Puritans, New England, the American Revolution and the United States ever since; and the sense of being a city upon a hill has remained at the core of American self-definition.[26]

From the beginning of the colony, care was taken to distance the leadership from the type of separatism found at Plymouth. Winthrop and other leaders felt that the Plymouth congregants had allowed so much freedom of opinion that discipline was wanting. This lack of discipline was best evidenced by the construction of the settlement known as Merry Mount, which a wayward Pilgrim by the name of Thomas Morton constructed. Merry Mount was founded in flagrant contrast to the strict modes of Puritan life, and life there included dancing around the pagan Maypole, drunkenness, cavorting with local Indian women, and the like. More dangerous to the Pilgrims, however, were the economic actions of Morton. Desiring to control the fur trade, he armed the Indians and taught them to shoot, a matter of concern to Plymouth both economically and militarily.

Winthrop and the men of Massachusetts Bay would tolerate no lack of conformity. Almost as soon as the colony was founded, two brothers by the name of Browne had a disagreement with the main church over issues pertaining to church liturgical practice. Their decision to start their own small congregation with individual practices led by conscience was met with resistance. The Brownes were summoned to a council, informed of the error of their ways, and returned to England. John Andrew Doyle, a colonial historian of the 1800s concludes that the Puritans had done the right thing in preventing the colony, right from the very outset, from becoming a haven for Separatists:

> If the colony was to become what its promoters intended, unity, not merely of religious belief, but of ritual and of ecclesiastical discipline, was, at least for the present, a needful condition of existence. We must not condemn the banishment of the Brownes unless we are prepared to say that it would have been better for the world if the Puritan colony of Massachusetts had never existed.[27]

George Ellis, a Puritan historian, makes the case that the Puritans were never Separatists, a charge from which Winthrop and others attempted to distance themselves regularly. Upon leaving for England less than a year before Winthrop, one of the Puritan ministers, Francis Higginson, provided instruction to his fellow travellers regarding their departure:

> We will not say, Farewell Babylon! Farewell Rome! But we will say, Farewell dear England! Farewell the Church of God in England, and all the Christian friends there! We do not go to New England as Separatists from the Church of England, though we cannot

---

[26] ""We Shall Be as a City upon a Hill"" Urban History Review 19, no. 1-2 (1990).

[27] Qtd. (What does this mean?) in George E. Ellis, The Puritan Age and Rule in the Colony of the Massachusetts Bay, 1629-1685 (Boston: Houghton Mifflin, 1888), 60.

but separate from the corruptions in it; but we go to practice the positive part of the Church reformation, and to propagate the Gospel in America.[28]

Instead, non-conformists is the preferred descriptor. Though the Puritans held to the doctrines of scripture and in those ways retained much of their similarity to the Church of England, it was the trappings of liturgy that they rejected.[29]

By 1637 Winthrop had lost an election and been reinstated as governor of Massachusetts. While some historians see his move toward independence from the religious authorities in the colony as one designed to increase his personal wealth and power, perhaps the previous seven years, with their infighting and occasional overruling of the magistrates, led John Winthrop to declare:

> Christ's kingdom is not of this world, therefore his officers of this kingdom cannot judicially inquire into affairs of the world. Such power would confound these jurisdictions, which Christ has made distinct, for as he is King of Kings and Lord of Lords, he has set up another kingdom in this world wherein magistrates are his officers and they are accountable to him.[30]

Winthrop was charged with achieving a delicate balance in the New World. He had many audiences, including the King of England, who expected loyalty, allegiance, and a profitable relationship with the colony, the various religious groups represented by the general term "Puritan" and even those outside of Puritanism, who were regularly seeking to assert themselves and their personally held doctrinal beliefs against the mainstream, his neighbors in Plymouth, often separatists with a host of infighting and resulting issues, as well as a source of both economic help and competition, and his fellow magistrates. Massachusetts Bay Colony has been referred to as a theocracy by some, but the name did not apply, at least at first. True, John Winthrop consulted church leaders on many of the Company's early decisions, but not until 1637 were the Massachusetts Bay Colony and the Puritan church fully integrated.

Chapter 4: The Great Migration

The greatest success of the Massachusetts Bay Colony would be its ability to attract a continuous stream of settlers to their shores. The failure of colonies in Canada and New Netherlands proved that no matter how advantageous the economics or how organized the leadership, numbers were the key to success in colonial settlement.[31] Unlike the Pilgrims, who had come to the New World earlier, but failed to attract further settlements and in fact had lost many of their settlers to both death and return to England, the Puritan settlement at Boston was an attractive place that saw huge growth almost immediately. The original 400 settlers had a

[28] Ellis, 55.
[29] Ibid., 62.
[30] Mark W. Crilly, "John Winthrop: Magistrate, Minister, Merchant," The Midwest Quarterly 40, no. 2 (1999).
[31] Morgan, 165.

terrible first year, as had the Pilgrims before them. Their recovery, however, and their unity, as demanded by Winthrop, was certainly remarkable. The good governance of the colony, combined with worsening conditions in England, meant that close to 20,000 people would come to Massachusetts Bay between 1630 and 1642. The Puritan settlements at Massachusetts Bay were unique in that "virtually from the beginning… the age structure and sex ratio in New England resembled those of established societies all over western Europe far more closely than was the case with any other new societies established by the English in America during the early modern era."[32] The settlement grew rapidly, not only due to the high immigration rates between 1630 and 1642, but also because of the relative long life expectancy and low infant mortality rates the Puritans at Massachusetts enjoyed.[33]

John Winthrop did not insist that all settlers be Puritan. He welcomed only those who were willing to follow the Puritan laws, however, saying, "When God gives a special commission; he looks to have it observed in every article."[34] Winthrop allowed, but did not agree with the Separatists. Separatists were public in their break from the Anglican Church and rejected it as impure. They were a group that had had constant problems and infighting since their arrival in the New World. Winthrop put this partially to the lack of authority among the Separatists and to their tendency to separate from any ecclesiastical authority whatsoever. Winthrop disagreed with the separatist's position, seeing it as "too exclusive and a failure of charity, it was dangerous because if Separatism became dominant, the bishops [of the Anglican Church] might get the king to revoke the Massachusetts Bay Charter."[35]

The Great Migration ended in 1640. For a short time, Massachusetts Bay experienced an economic downturn as the income and cash flow from the old world ebbed.[36] Conditions in England had changed, as Charles I, the great persecutor of the Protestant Puritans, was put to death in 1649. Oliver Cromwell began to rule England in a Puritan "protectorate" in 1653, disrupting the line of Kings. His regard for Puritanism was high, but he allowed other Christian sects, even Catholics, to worship in the Protectorate. Less persecution meant fewer Puritans fleeing their home country for the New World. Cromwell himself held the New World in low regard, calling New England "poor, cold, and useless."[37]

Chapter 5: Economy

A history of the New England colonies: Plymouth, Rhode Island, Connecticut, New Hampshire, and Massachusetts is in many ways a history of the Massachusetts Bay Colony, so great was its influence on the colonies that surrounded or broke away from it. Conditions in

---

[32] Jack P. Greene, *Pursuits of Happiness: The Social Development of Early Modern British Colonies and the Formation of American Culture* (Chapel Hill, NC: University of North Carolina Press, 1988), 19.

[33] Ibid., 20.

[34] Dillon, 209.

[35] Ibid.

[36] Taylor, 175.

[37] Ibid.

Massachusetts and the surrounding areas were favorable for long term growth and attracted settlement. Despite the end of the Great Migration, the New England area had 30,000 settlers in 1660, but over 90,000 by 1700.[38]

While the overwhelming historiography of Massachusetts Bay colony and New England has shown that the Puritans were the most successful in transplanting the English life they had to the New World, maintaining their economic positions and their social structures, some recent scholars claim that the Puritans of the Great Migration feared the economic and social changes that were taking place in England and fled to the Americas to avoid the change, creating a tightly controlled society in the name of morality and religion.[39] Casey Pratt, a libertarian economist, argues that despite the religious intensity of the founders, "economic scarcity was the rule right from the inception of the colony in Massachusetts, and in spite of their very earnest focus on spiritual matters, the Puritans could not altogether neglect the natural, material world."[40] Historians who disagree see not a conflict between the spiritual and economic concerns of the founders of the colony, but a lack of understanding of their view of both: "The Puritans understood in spiritual terms many causes we might define as 'economic.' They interpreted the wandering beggars, cloth trade depression, and famines [of England] as divine afflictions meant to punish a guilty land that wallowed in sin."[41]

Both sides of the historiographical debate agree that the settlers of New England provided a great contrast to those English colonists in other areas, including the Chesapeake region and Ireland. Both Virginian and Irish colonists had weaker family structures, an abundance of unskilled male laborers, little knowledge of farming in the areas in which they now lived, and (to a greater degree in Virginia) had to have external controls such as martial law in order to maintain discipline and order. Though Bermuda had a high concentration of Puritans, the cash crop culture and the plurality of religions as well as the absence of the important social institutions of Puritan schools and legal systems meant that despite its Puritan majority, it would not achieve the cohesiveness of New England's Bay Colony.[42] These areas also allowed for a greater chance for social mobility in both positive and negative directions.[43]

The relative income of Massachusetts Bay settlers was far more equitable than that of other regions, such as Virginia. The climate of Massachusetts Bay did not lend itself to a particular cash crop. There was no blockbuster agricultural product that was likely to cause a settler to become a rich man overnight, unlike the tobacco, indigo, and rice crops of the south. Instead, the people of Massachusetts Bay were generally farmers and raisers of cattle, as well as fisherman, timber man, and fur traders.[44] The crops and products produced by the Massachusetts Bay

---

[38] Greene, 56.

[39] Ibid., 36-38.

[40] Casey Pratt, "Roger Williams's Unintentional Contribution to the Creation of American Capitalism," *Libertarian Papers* 3 (2011).

[41] Taylor, 167.

[42] Ibid., 42-3.

[43] Ibid. 41.

community were widely diverse, including "wheat, rye, oats, peas, barley, beef, pork, fish, butter, cheese, timber, mast, tar, sope, plankboard, frames of houses, clapboards, and pipe staves."[45] The wide variety of products was mostly produced for the community itself, who rather than living by subsistence on their farms alone, would have the standard of living to which they had been accustomed by trading and bartering these goods with one another. Export of fish, beef and pork, wood, and whale products would become common by 1770. Puritans sought a standard of living they called "independent competency." The Puritans believed strongly in the dignity of the individual. Competency meant that a family would have work, adequate food and clothing, shelter, education, and that this level of prosperity would pass on to their children.[46] Rather than the extremes between rich and poor they had witnessed in England, Massachusetts Bay Puritans believed that "nothing sorts better with Piety than Competency."[47] While some historians see the upper-middle class dominance of Massachusetts Bay leaders as a tendency toward oligarchy with mercantilism as its foundation, it is more likely that the Puritans sought not a society of economic equals, but one of spiritual focus rather than concentration on amassing New World fortunes. Their "sameness" came not from economic philosophy by design at least, but as a result of their spiritual goals.

The economic depression of the 1640s, caused by the slowdown in new settlement and available cash, caused new industries to develop. The fishing industry took root along the coastlines, but not amongst the original Puritan settlers. Fishing attracted immigrants from the old world and the hard lifestyle and working conditions were not conducive to traditional families or to the constitutions of the middle class Puritans. Indeed, the kind of men who began to come to New England to fish and make their fortunes presented a moral challenge to the Bay Colony. Alan Taylor records an incident in which a Puritan preacher visited a fishing village with a reminder about the purpose of the colony in the New World, to glorify God. "Sir," the fisherman replied, "You think you are preaching to the people of Massachusetts Bay, our main end was to catch fish."[48] The tension between the colonies' original purposes and economic growth is a subject of interest for historians who debate whether these were mutually exclusive, and therefore competing forces, or whether good economics was part and parcel with Puritan spiritual life.

The new industries of the 1640s thrived in part as a result of problems in England. With an English Civil War and the disruption of the monarchy, Massachusetts Bay and its surrounding areas could supply markets with fish, timber, and ships that were needed. Labor costs were more expensive in the New World than in England, but resources were far cheaper, making them competitive enough to cause later English merchants to complain about the colony's economic purpose in terms of its diversity from established English industry. Many English fisherman and

Comment [PE]: Do ou mean "soap?"

---

[44] Greene, 25.
[45] Taylor, 176.
[46] Ibid., 172.
[47] Ibid.
[48] Ibid., 175.

ship-builders believed that an internal competitor was dangerous to their businesses and resented the thriving economy of Massachusetts Bay.[49]

Chapter 6: Family Life

Life in Massachusetts Bay was prosperous, but only because of the commitment of the entire family to work and flourish in the New World. Family life revolved around work and dedication to God, which were viewed as one and the same. The division of labor was somewhat traditional in that men were responsible for hard labor and women tended to the house and gardens, as well as the production of household goods. Despite this, Puritan theologians tended to take an unorthodox view of the marital division of roles, believing that the partner best suited for a particular task should be given responsibility over it. Women, therefore had a more prominent role in Massachusetts Bay than in other colonies. When a spouse was away, a wife was to assume the role of "deputy husband."[50]

Puritan marriages were not only economic partnerships, but "romantic" ones.[51] Parents did not seek to arrange marriages between their children, but let the children take the lead in suggesting a marriage, with the understanding that parents could reject an unwise match. Puritans took their doctrine seriously, and this meant that men as well as women were subject to the church's critique. Men were called to love their wives, as the scriptures admonished. Those who were abusive or neglectful could be expected to come under the discipline of the church, which saw these actions as a violation of both the scripture and of the community of believers. Divorce on Biblical grounds of abandonment or adultery, therefore, was more easily obtained in Massachusetts Bay than in England.[52] Though different in the sexual division of roles in some ways, Massachusetts Bay was orthodox in others; women could not hold public office, could not be ministers, and could not own or inherit property, with the exception of widows. [53]

Literacy in the Massachusetts Bay colony was of chief importance. The Puritans who founded the colony desired to leave many of the traditions of the old world behind. This included religious ceremonies and feast days that the Anglican Church promoted, many with an original purpose of illustrating Biblical concepts for poor and illiterate congregants. The Puritans, on the other hand, believed that every man, woman, and child should have access to the scriptures, and therefore, that reading was key to the fulfillments of their spiritual mission. Not only the Bible, but other texts would aid the Puritans in knowing more about their God and the world he had created. This belief led to several factors that made Massachusetts Bay and her ever-growing and surrounding communities unique: most settlers owned a Bible and other books, nearly every town had an established grammar school for the instruction of children, and all churches had a

---

[49] Ibid., 178.
[50] Ibid., 173.
[51] Ibid.
[52] Ibid.
[53] Ibid.

college-educated minster who could expect his aides to be challenged by parishioners who regularly read both the Bible and books of theology.[54]

Chapter 7: Indian Relations

Soon after their arrival, the Puritans had begun to experience economic success. Persecution of Puritans in England by Charles I meant that Puritans would continue to arrive in Massachusetts and would join their economic fortunes to the colony. In a short time, they outpaced their Pilgrim brothers in establishing trade posts and taking over the established traded relations that the Pilgrims had with local Indians. Seven years into the founding of the Massachusetts Bay colony, their rapid expansion would come to war.

John Winthrop recorded his first contact with the Pequots when he was visited by a Pequot trader bearing gifts in 1634. The Pequot requested that the English act as negotiators in their ongoing dispute with the Narragansett Indians, who had strong alliances with the Dutch. In exchange for English help and protection, the Pequot would exclusively trade with the English and would encourage the English to safely settle in the area of Connecticut.[55] The Puritans rejected the exclusive treaty as well as the call to defend the Pequot in their disputes with the Narragansett, but did enter into a trade treaty with the Pequot. One of the key issues that prevented further cooperation between the Puritans and the Pequot was the murder of an English trade ship captain by the name of John Stone.

The Pequot Indians had murdered two English trade captains in retribution for the killing of Sachems by Dutch traders, whom they had mistaken for Englishmen. At the treaty negotiations taking place in 1634, the Puritans demanded that the Pequot deliver the guilty parties to Massachusetts Bay for the sake of justice. Originally, the Pequot negotiators attempted to explain their confusion between the English and Dutch traders, as well as to claim that Captain Stone had been irresponsible in his actions, having taken two Indians as captives just before the Indian attack.[56] Much later, at the point of attack, the Pequot representative would make a final effort to claim that the killing of Stone had been a case of mistaken revenge: "We know no difference between the Dutch and the English, they are both strangers to us, we took them all to be one; therefore, we crave pardon, we have not willfully wronged the English."[57]

John Winthrop appeared to believe the Pequot had acted in good faith after this discussion, saying that the Pequot version of events "was related with such confidence and gravity, as, having no means to contradict, we were inclined to believe it" and relating to Plymouth's William Bradford that the killing of Captain Stone had taken place during a "just quarrel."[58]

---

[54] Ibid., 179.
[55] Alfred A. Cave, The Pequot War (Amherst, MA: University of Massachusetts Press, 1996), 70-1.
[56] Ibid. 71.
[57] Ibid., 115.
[58] Ibid. 72.

The Puritans were no strangers to the character of John Stone. Stone was a notorious trade captain and sometimes pirate who had earned a reputation as a fearless tradesman in Europe. Already, Stone had caused trouble in both Massachusetts Bay and in Plymouth, having led citizens to public brawls, drunkenness, and falling just shy of conviction of adultery with a woman of Massachusetts Bay. Stone had been subjected to a heavy fine from the Bay Colony and no one mourned his death when word reached the colony that he had been killed by Indians.[59] Massachusetts Bay's Roger Clap recorded his feelings on the news in his memoir: "Thus did God destroy him that proudly threatened to ruin us, by complaining against us when he came to England. Thus God destroyed him, and delivered us at that time also."[60]

Winthrop's diary later records that though the civil authorities of Massachusetts Bay did not feel the need for the Pequot to turn over Stone's killers, the religious authorities, with whom the government regularly consulted, demanded it. Therefore, the 1634 treaty conditions included the expedition of the guilty Pequot to the colonial authorities[61] and this led to a declaration of war by the Puritans on the Pequot's.[62]

The Puritans believed that God would prosper their war on the Pequot's. They also, however, negotiated with other Indian tribes, hoping to exploit the differences between warring groups to their advantage. Thus, the Narragansett Indians helped the Puritans in their raiding of a Pequot village that killed over 400 men, women, and children.

John Underhill led the men of Massachusetts Bay in the fight against the Pequot, avenging the death of John Oldham, another tradesman whom they suspected the Pequot had killed. There has been much debate as to the real killers of Oldham, whose body was found on his sloop with a group of Narragansett Indians. Some theories credit the killing of Oldham to the Narragansett, and others to the Pequot, whom they say sheltered the killers as they fled from the English. When the Massachusetts Bay magistrates heard of the death of Oldham, the issue of Stone's murder remained unresolved. To many of the Puritans, this second death seemed to confirm that any hesitation on their part to seek retribution for English deaths would lead to bolder attacks. A "preemptive strike" was the best answer they could give.[63]

---

[59] Ibid., 73-74.
[60] Ibid., 74.
[61] Ibid. 75.
[62] I bid., 178.
[63] Ibid., 109.

Bust of John Underhill

After an unsuccessful attack on the Pequot of Block Island, Underhill set sail to find a Pequot village, recording in his journal the Pequot greetings to which he and his men made no answer, "What cheer, Englishmen, what cheer, what do you come for?" They, not thinking we intended war, went on cheerfully until they came to Pequeat River."[64] The Pequot, in fear of an English attack, began to negotiate an alliance with the Narragansett, a friendship that would have certainly upset the balance of power in the favor of the Indians. The Massachusetts Bay Colony was desperate enough to call on Roger Williams, who had been banned from the Bay, yet negotiated with the Narragansett and prevented the alliance with the Pequot. For his work in saving the English, John Winthrop suggested that Roger William's banishment be rescinded, but he was outvoted by the council.[65]

To Underhill, the victory of Massachusetts Bay men over the Indians was a miracle of sorts, and certainly a blessing sent by God. He describes his enemies as:

> ...that insolent and barbarous nation called the Pequeats, whom by the sword of the Lord, and a few feeble instruments, soldiers not accustomed to war, were drove out of their country, and slain by the sword, to the number of fifteen hundred souls, in the space of two months and less; so as their country is fully subdued and fallen into the hands of

---

[64] Ibid., 114.
[65] Ibid., 125.

the English. And to the end that God's name might have the glory, and his people see his power, and magnify his honor for his great goodness.[66]

Underhill records that representatives of the Pequots admitted to the killings of two English trade ship captains, but defended themselves as having carried out the killings as retribution for an earlier fatal attack on one of their sachems. The Pequots claimed that they saw the Dutch and English as one people, and had not realized that the men who killed their sachem during a trade dispute had been from a different country completely. Interestingly, Underhill makes no comment on these words, launching instead into a description of the attack that followed on the Pequot fort. Both the Puritan settlers and the Indians recoiled at the sights and sounds of slaughter, and some questioned the severity of the response, but Underhill ultimately defended the actions in response to the question,

> Should not Christians have more mercy and compassion? But I would refer you to David's war. When a people is grown to such a height of blood, and sin against God and man, and all confederates in the action, there he hath no respect to persons, but harrows them, and saws them, and puts them to the sword, and the most terriblest death that may be. Sometimes the Scripture declareth women and children must perish with their parents. Sometimes the case alters; but we will not dispute it now. We had sufficient light from the word of God for our proceedings.[67]

Indians were exposed to much Christian teaching, especially by the Puritan missionaries who attempted to engage and convert them. "Praying towns" were settlements where Indian converts could be controlled and their morality monitored. Historian Daniel Richter compares the effectiveness of the praying towns to the Jesuit missions of the western America and the French Catholic settlements and finds both wanting in terms of creating an "indigenous Puritan leadership" in the New World. About 2,300 Native Americans lived in the Massachusetts praying towns by 1674.[68]

---

[66] John Underhill. "The Pequot Wars". *Connecticut History on the Web.*

[67] Ibid.

[68] Daniel Richter. *Facing East from the Indian Country: A Native History of Early America.* Cambridge: Harvard University Press. 2001. 95.

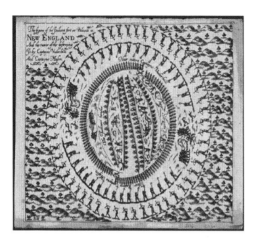

An Engraving from Underhill's Account of the Pequot War, Showing an Assault on a Pequot Fort

Chapter 8: Memoir of Roger Clap

Roger Clap was a young man when he arrived in Massachusetts Bay in 1630. His memoir of the founding of the colony was recorded when he reached his seventies, as a spiritual legacy to his descendants- a "telling of His wondrous works," as he put it.[69] Clap's diary records first-hand accounts of the Bay's founding as well as of his experiences with Indian groups. First, he records how the captain of the ship he arrived on refused to enter the Charles River, instead dropping the arriving Puritan settlers off at Nantasket, to "shift for ourselves."[70] Clap's group grew skittish when they came upon a company of over 300 Indians, but described how the Indians did not come near them, and instead appeared to offer a bass fish to the men they had come upon. In return, Clap's group "sent a man with a biscuit and changed the cake for the bass. Afterwards, they supplied us with bass, exchanging a bass for a biscuit cake, and were very friendly unto us."[71]

Clap describes the initial year of his Massachusetts Bay experience as a difficult one, filled with hunger as a result of a very limited diet. Having arrived too late for the planting season, the people of Massachusetts Bay seemed to suffer most from their want of bread, and to a secondary degree meat. Through fishing, the settlers provided themselves with "clams and mussels and fish,"[72] and foreign ships and trade with local Indians were relied upon for other foods important

---

[69] Roger Clap. "Surviving the First Year of the Massachusetts Bay Colony, 1630-1631". *National Humanities Center Resource Toolbox.*

[70] Ibid.

[71] Ibid.

[72] Ibid.

Comment [PE]: Do you mean Nantucket?

for survival. Clap recounts the provision to the settlers as the mercy of God and credits the wisdom of the colony's leaders in seeing that ship goods were made available to men "as they had need,"[73] but also cautions his readers to ask themselves whether or not they, now beneficiaries to Massachusetts Bay's great economic success, had not better bellies, but better hearts than their forefathers.[74]

Chapter 9: Dealing with Dissent

The Puritans of Massachusetts Bay did not welcome those from other religious faiths, proclaiming that Baptists, Catholics, Quakers, and others had "free Liberty to keep away from us."[75] The uniformity of denomination they sought, however, never produced a unity of thought. The Puritans, no matter whether looking at the founding generation or in generations to come, were never short on internal controversy amongst the churches and minsters of the Bay. Alan Taylor puts this tendency in part to the "cosmic stakes"[76] which, in the Puritans view, were at hand in almost every matter of religion and practice.

In the years 1630 to 1631, the leadership of Massachusetts Bay banished 14 people from the colony, a number which author Nan Goodman points out was "an astonishing 1.4 percent of the population."[77] She presents the case of Roger Williams' banishment as not simply a religious, but a legal conflict that resulted in a protracted discussion between Williams and John Cotton, lasting over 15 years. For Goodman, this discussion has immense historical implications in understanding not only the religious dynamics of the Massachusetts Bay Colony, but its legal position in terms of its residents, their status as citizens of England and the New World, and the definitions of both church and state authority.[78] Seeing the ongoing argument over Williams' punishments as "nothing less than a debate between religious and common-law notions of identity"[79] gives pause to those who would view the banishment of Roger Williams, Anne Hutchinson, and others as merely church discipline, as exercised by the Puritan church.

Chapter 10: Anne Hutchinson

Anne Hutchinson's history of controversy in Massachusetts Bay history is of no surprise considering her father, Francis Marbury. Marbury, educated at Cambridge and an ordained deacon in the Church of England, was a thorn in the side of his superiors from the moment he took his position. His vocal criticism of the clergy and the inept leadership that placed them in power led to Marbury serving several short jail terms, enduring a period of house arrest, and suffering two years in prison after a judgment handed to him by the Bishop of London. His

---

[73] Ibid.
[74] Ibid.
[75] Taylor, 181.
[76] Ibid., 182.
[77] Nan Goodman, "Banishment, Jurisdiction, and Identity in Seventeenth-Century New England: The Case of Roger Williams," Early American Studies 7, no. 1 (2009).
[78] Ibid.
[79] Ibid.

outspoken and abrasive manner clearly influenced his daughter Anne. His ideas became her ideas. His personality shaped hers.[80] From 1636 to 1638 she was embroiled in the Antinomian controversy of the Massachusetts Bay Colony.

Hutchinson's family relocated to London as a result of her father's burned bridges in Northamptonshire and then chance appointment to a position in London in 1605.[81] As Hutchinson was being raised in London, she was routinely exposed to the world of religious controversy. Her home was a place for religious debate, [82] and intense scrutiny of church leadership was not prohibited.[83] Anne Hutchinson mirrored her father's love for both religious controversy and criticism of church leadership. Soon after she was married, Anne and her husband William settled in Alford, a town in England about 25 miles from old Boston, where a young preacher, John Cotton, was ministering at St. Botolphs.[84]

Reverend John Cotton

Anne would soon discover that her strong beliefs aligned with Cotton's teaching. Cotton

---

[80] Winnifred King Rugg.*Unafraid: A Life of Anne Hutchinson* (Boston: Houghton Mifflin, 1930), 22.
[81] Ibid., 23.
[82] Ibid., 21.
[83] Ibid., 24.
[84] Ibid., 38

echoed her father's words, and so, whenever opportunity afforded, on a Sunday morning, or a midweek class, Anne consumed as many of Cotton's lectures as possible.[85] Though there was a common ground she felt with Cotton, it was not without internal conflict. Her support for Cotton was unwavering, and because she had given herself over to his instruction, her close proximity to Cotton's ministry brought her pause as she observed small changes being made with the liturgy of the church. These changes were stripping away the rites even her reform-minded father observed.[86] Cotton drew fire from church magistrates because he refused to conform to proper liturgy and regulations set by the church and the church leadership responded to Cotton's infractions by giving him the choice to conform or leave. Cotton chose to leave, and Anne was devastated.[87] As time passed, Mr. Cotton's absence cultivated an ever-increasing dissatisfaction with her local clergy. Hutchinson pressed her husband, William, to consider the colony in America where Mr. Cotton relocated. Her impassioned speeches regarding religious freedom and spiritual utopia were unrelenting. William resisted at first, but his arguments were eclipsed by his wife's stubborn resolve. She was convinced that God had told her to seek out the pure teaching of men who would speak boldly in the face of religious persecution.[88]

William, Anne, and their children set sail for Boston in the summer of 1634. Within two years Hutchinson had well developed social connections throughout Massachusetts Bay. Her previous connection to John Cotton and their renewed friendship gave her much weight in the community. William's ambitions also played a role in aiding Hutchinson's influence. His success as a businessman and position as deputy of the court bolstered her status with those of influence.[89]

Among the women of Massachusetts Bay, Anne Hutchinson was a confidant. She was regularly sought out for advice and spiritual guidance. This led to what was quite possibly the first club for women in America.[90] The women's club was as fertile ground as any for Hutchinson's influence and ideas about proper living and the doctrine of the church in everyday life. The women met in her home once a week, and quickly grew to twice a week as the number attending outpaced the capacity of her home. As Hutchinson followed in her father's footsteps, her opinions on Christian doctrine and criticisms of the church drew a wider audience.[91] At one point she submitted her bother-in-law's name for official church ministry in the colony. He was rejected by colonial leadership because of his doctrinal beliefs. This infuriated Hutchinson and divided Boston between those who supported her and those who supported John Winthrop.[92]

As the people of Boston took sides, the lines were drawn for what became known as the

---

[85] Ibid., 39-40
[86] Ibid., 44-46
[87] Ibid., 47
[88] Ibid.,-60
[89] Ibid., 79.
[90] Ibid., 92.
[91] Ibid., 103-104.
[92] Ibid., 102-103.

Antinomian controversy. The Antinomian controversy surrounded two primary Christian doctrines. John Cotton, Governor Henry Vane, and Anne Hutchinson believed that all Christians have the indwelling of the Holy Spirit. A person's status before God was not based upon spiritual works, but on legal grounds, having been justified through Christ. The ideas that Christians were not guilty before God, despite sinful actions and thoughts,[93] caused others to fear these teachings, believing that a rejection of the Law of God in the Old Testament was what was being implied. Hutchinson, along with those who believed in this doctrine, was disparagingly called "antinomian." Antinomian means an opposition to literalism. For those in the established Puritan church of Anne Hutchinson's time, it meant rejecting the literal "Law" of the Old Testament for the spiritual "Gospel of the New."[94] The spiritual disciplines as taught by Hutchinson were not something that manifested in one's external life, but rather were an internal phenomenon based on the work of God. The religious leaders in Boston did not hesitate to express their confusion, disdain, and frustration with the antinomian position. If a person was a follower of Christ and a Christian, then there naturally should be external markers in that person's life that set them apart as a Christian.[95] As the controversy over antinomianism spread, John Winthrop saw the potential threat this group, and subsequent splinter groups, were to the charter for the Massachusetts Bay colony. To avoid trouble with England, he set out to restrict what people read, where they went for entertainment, and how they spent their time in order to preserve religious and moral orthodoxy.[96]

The rivalry that developed between Hutchinson and her neighbor John Winthrop was, in the view of feminist historian Cheryl Smith, an issue of Hutchinson's growing power and influence. As a well-respected mother of 14, a mid-wife and healer, and a person looked to by many for advice and interpretation of scripture, Hutchinson, for Smith, represented a challenge to the existing power structure.[97] Her view, as well as others, paints the Massachusetts Bay authorities as seeking to quiet, at all costs, a woman who dared to speak against the civil and religious authorities of the colony. This interpretation of events can be challenged by a consideration of the trial and similar fate of Roger Williams, an educated male of Massachusetts Bay.

In 1637 at the age of 46, Anne found herself on trial for dissension within the colony and churches. After days of argumentation and deliberation, Anne was found guilty and banished from the colony. The trial was recorded, and Hutchinson can be seen defending herself vigorously in the initial civil trial. Nonetheless, the governor handed down the sentence: "It is that you are banished from out our jurisdiction as being a woman not fit for our society. And you are to be imprisoned till the Court send you away."[98] By claiming, while on trial, that "the voice

[93] Ibid.
[94] Ibid., 112.
[95] Ibid. 115.
[96] Ibid., 121-122.
[97] Cheryl C. Smith, "Out of Her Place: Anne Hutchinson and the Dislocation of Power in New World Politics," Journal of American Culture (Malden, MA) 29, no. 4 (2006)
[98] Rugg, 183.

of [God's] own spirit [spoke] to my soul"[99], Hutchinson brought about not only her civil banishment, but her excommunication from the church from the Puritan church. John Cotton distanced himself from Hutchinson in the final trial held by church authorities.[100]

Hutchinson on Trial

The pregnant Hutchinson was banished from both colony and church, had a stillborn child in exile (which in some minds was further evidence of her sinful ways)[101] and was killed by Indians while living in a Dutch settlement in 1643.[102] Hutchinson was influential, but she did not serve as an official minister of the Puritan church as did another who would also run afoul of the Puritan desire for conformity.

Chapter 10: Roger Williams

Roger Williams arrived in Massachusetts Bay in 1631. He was a young minister, and one with plenty of ideas, some of which appeared to be original, not a positive characteristic to the

---

[99] Smith.

[100] Ibid.

[101] Ibid.

[102] Sandra F. VanBurkleo. "To be rooted Out of Her Station: The Ordeal of Anne Hutchinson". American Political Trials, ed. Michal R. Belknap. (Westport, CT: Praeger Publishers, 1994).

Puritans and Winthrop. Upon his arrival in Massachusetts Bay, Winthrop referred to Williams as "a godly minister,"[103] but the two were to have dealings that would bring them into both conflicts an occasional aid and friendship over the years to come. Events to come may have been foreshadowed by Williams' refusal to heed the call of the Boston church to be its pastor on the grounds that, having examined the congregation, they were not a "separated people." At only 28, it would surely have been advantageous to Williams and his family to take the position in the growing church. Instead, Williams answered the call of the tempestuous Salem church, a call which the Puritan leaders opposed. Williams served as an assistant to the main teacher at Salem, a place where he felt he could freely express himself on matters of conscience and where he continued to express his dismay at the loyalty he felt existed to the Church of England among the Puritans at Boston.[104] Eventually Williams' developing conscience led him to reject even the saints at Plymouth, since they were officially non-separatists. As "the first important rigid separatist in New England,"[105] Roger Williams had lived among the settlers he would eventually come to reject, learning farming and welcoming Indians to his land and property. These would be important lessons later, as Williams was determined to live amongst and become a missionary to the Indian tribes of New England. "My desire is," he said, "that I may intent what I long after, the Native's Soul."[106]

Salem Church issued a second call to Williams in 1632, which he took and which put him back under the authority of Massachusetts Bay. On this second time in Salem, Williams' tension with the Massachusetts Bay leadership increased. The Plymouth church was divided, with some members wishing Williams to stay; as a result, when Williams departed for Salem Church, he took several Plymouth members with him.[107] The Salem church was now in agreement with Roger Williams ever more radical ideas - including the idea that the King had no right to give away land that belonged to the Indians and therefore all colonial charters granted by England were invalid, that an oath taken by a non-Christian was invalid, since oaths were before God, and that the church magistrates had no jurisdiction over one's relationship to God as defined in the first four commandments:[108] "Hence I affirm it lamentably to be against the Testimony of Christ Jesus, for the civil state to impose upon the souls of the people, a religion, a worship, a ministry, oaths (in religious and civil affairs), tithes, times, days, marryings and buryings in holy ground." Instead the state should give "free and absolute permission of conscience to all men in what is merely spiritual. . . and provide for the liberty of the magistrate's conscience also."

William's criticism of the Bay colony continued. He grew to be considered a great danger to the colony because of his influence on Puritans who remained in England and his overt belief that the charters granted to the Bay colony were actually invalid. According to Williams, the

---

[103] James Ernst, Roger Williams, New England Firebrand (New York: Macmillan, 1932), 61.
[104] Ernst, 74-77.
[105] Ernst, 75.
[106] Ibid., 77.
[107] Emily Easton, *Roger Williams: Prophet and Pioneer* (Boston: Houghton, Mifflin, 1930), 154.
[108] Ibid., 164.

Comment [PE]: I find this part of the sentence confusing.

Comment [PE]: Is "intent" the correct word here?

Comment [PE]: I cannot find these two words in the dictionary - marryings and buryings.

charter could give the colonists the right only to trade, not to settle the lands which properly belonged to the Indians. Not long after Salem's second call, Williams began being summoned to Massachusetts Bay to answer for his utterances on the lack of validity of the colonial land claims and how church or government –administered oaths were sinful in that they caused the unregenerate to swear to God falsely.[109] Finally, the ecclesiastical court called Roger Williams to repentance for his general lack of obedience to the church leadership and his many dangerous opinions. He was given time to consider the charges and to consult with the leadership of the Salem church which was now also being called out for its error by the other churches. Attempts by the leaders of Massachusetts Bay to reason with Williams failed. Eventually, Roger Williams, in a fast day sermon, publicly accused Massachusetts Bay of the following sins:

- acknowledging the King's patent claiming right to America by discovery and Christianity
- the Bay's sin in claiming right thereby to Indian lands
- the magistrates punishing for breach of the First Tables
- enforced church attendance
- unseparated churches in the Bay and at Plymouth
- national church of England as anti-Christian
- the enforcing of civil oaths
- the meeting of the clergy as tending to presbytery
- the church having "a Christ without a Cross"
- the treaty with the Pequot tribe[110]

By 1637, Williams was banned from Massachusetts. His trial came about only after protracted arguments amongst Williams, the Salem church, the civil authorities of the Bay colony and others about the propriety of prosecution, which Williams claimed was invalid since he was acting on conscience, and his disagreement was with the church, not the civil authority of the colony. The Bay colony's answer to this was that "in religious and civil affairs the church was the highest authority. The Bible was the source of all law and justice. The state was merely the civil arm used by the Puritan church to carry out her decrees and penalties."[111] The disagreement between Williams and the Puritan leadership was essentially one of doctrine, revolving first around the question of the proper division between church and civil authority. As Alan Taylor explains: "The merger of the church and state in service to a hierarchical social order gave political significance to every religious issue. The combination obliged dissidents to express their social and political grievances in religious rhetoric, and it made social and political critics of those seeking religious purity."[112]

---

[109] Easton, 166.
[110] Ernst, 107.
[111] Ibid., 127.
[112] Taylor, 160.

The trial was held without formal charges or an attorney for Williams, but a statement by the court of Williams' beliefs was made, with which Williams agreed, saying "the particulars were rightly held up."[113] Williams held that:

- "...We have not our land by Patent from the King but that the Natives are the true owners of it and that we ought to repent of such a receiving it by Patent."
- "That it is not lawful to call a wicked person to swear, to pray, as being actions of God's worship."
- "That it is not lawful to hear any of the ministers of the parish assemblies in England."
- "That the civil magistrate's power extends only to the bodies and goods and outward state of man."[114]

Both John Cotton and John Winthrop were later to argue that these beliefs were not, in fact, what Williams was banished for, but instead for his great disruption to the colony and church in arguing for these principles and attempting to win over others to his cause in disruptive manners:

> For if he had not looked upon himself as one that had received a clearer illumination and apprehension of the state of Christ's Kingdom and of the purity of church communion than all Christendom besides, he would never have taken upon himself as usually his manner was, to give public advertisement and admonition to all men whether of meaner or more public note and place of the corruptions of religion which himself observed in their judgments and practices.[115]

The trial went on for the entire day of October 8, 1635, during which, ironically, the religious ministers attempted to prevent the banishment of Williams. He was called upon to soften his stance, to repent, not of his beliefs but of the strident and disruptive way he had held them, but Williams could not be convinced, proclaiming he was ready "not only to be bound and banished, but to die also in New England" if necessary. The following morning, the 50 minsters present voted, with all but one, John Cotton, voting for Williams' banishment from the Colony. [116] Williams was given six weeks to leave the colony and charged not to return without permission. Williams petitioned the Colony to allow him to stay until the coming spring, on the basis of his illness and exhaustion, his wife's impending delivery, and the coming winter. An extension was granted, providing that Williams did not use the time granted to attempt to win others over to his position. Williams was cut off from communication with his former church at Salem, which now realized the error of its association with Williams. Williams continued to preach, holding services at his home. These services attracted his loyalists, and a plan soon hatched for the founding of a new colony in Narragansett, with land having been procured by Williams in a

---

[113] Ibid, 130.
[114] Ibid.
[115] John Cotton qtd.in Ernst, 132.
[116] Ibid., 133.

Comment [PE]: Should this be "of" instead of "to?"

treaty with the Wampanoag and Narragansett tribes. This again, attracted the attention of civil authorities, since Williams was in direct violation of the conditions of his extension. The colony called for Williams to be sent to England for trial, despite his appeal on the ground that he was too sick to come to Boston to dispute the new charges or be placed on a ship for England. By this time, John Winthrop, who, though he had voted for Williams's banishment, had been censured by Massachusetts Bay for being too lenient upon wayward souls. At Winthrop's advice, Williams had been gone from his home for three days before the council sent from Massachusetts Bay to arrest him arrived.[117] Williams journeyed alone, having left his wife and children behind, to the settlements of Narragansett Indians, finding lodging where he could that winter. His words regarding his winter banishment remain for those who debate the validity of his banishment to examine:

> I was unmercifully driven from my chamber to a winter's flight, exposed to the miseries, poverties, necessities, wants, debts, hardships of sea and land in a banished condition. It lies upon Massachusetts and me to examine with fear and trembling before the eyes of flaming fire the true cause of all my sorrow and suffering. . . Between those my friends of the Bay and Plymouth, I was sorely tossed for one fourteen weeks in a bitter winter season, not knowing what bread and bed did mean. . . I desire it may be seriously reviewed by all men 'that one beloved in Christ' as Mr. Cotton wrote, 'be denied the common air to breathe in and a civil cohabitation . . . yea, and also without mercy and humane compassion be exposed to a winter's miseries in a howling wilderness of frost and snow. . . A monstrous paradox that God's children should persecute God's children and that they hope to live together eternally with Christ Jesus in the heavens should not suffer each other to live in this common air together.'[118]

Religious controversy continued in the Bay colony after the banishments of Hutchinson and Williams. Thomas Hooker, at whose church the trial had been held, moved with his followers to Connecticut, eventually founding a new colony. The Salem church continued to divide and fight amongst themselves, and the Plymouth church requested that Williams move completely out of their area, along with the dissenters that had joined him in the spring of 1636. Finally, in May of 1636, Williams and his crew began to build what would become Providence, Rhode Island.[119]

---

[117] Ibid., 153.
[118] Ibid., 156.
[119] Ibid., 163.

Narragansett Indians Receiving Roger Williams

Chapter 11: The End of Massachusetts Bay

By 1662, the conformity to Puritan doctrine and morality had declined. The second generation of Massachusetts Bay settlers had been invited into the church as members through the "half-way covenant," a compromise that allowed Massachusetts Bay residents to become members of the church without even claiming a conversion experience, but only on the basis that they had been baptized as infants.[120] Later, Solomon Stoddard, the grandfather of Great Awakening preacher Jonathan Edwards opined "that a pure membership was a flimsy foundation on which to construct an ecclesiastical system, and that the restraining influence of the church on the entire community was more important than the preservation of a [pure] congregation of saints."[121]

Historians disagree in their interpretation of the Massachusetts Bay of the late seventeenth century. For some, the second half of the century suggests "declension," a period of moral decline and drift from the colony's purpose. Other historians deny the declension model, arguing that much of the evidence used to support declension comes from the Puritans own self-criticism. Therefore, rather than indicating a lack of purpose of failing morality in the colony, the testimony of the Puritans is evidence of their continued faith and for their concern that the colony remain a "city on a hill." The writings under debate are largely a particular style of sermon that appeared in the 1640s called the Jeremiad. Named for the weeping Old Testament prophet Jeremiah, these sermons lamented the state of affairs and hearts of a wayward people, sought to

---

[120] Greene, 58.
[121] Ibid.

warn them of their failings, called for a return to spiritual vigilance. The frequency of the Jeremiad grew rapidly: "In the 1640s there commenced in the sermons of New England a lament over the waning of primitive zeal and the consequent atrophy of public morals, which swelled to an incessant chant within forty years. By 1680 there seems to have been hardly any other theme for discourse."[122]

Author of *American Colonies*, Alan Taylor, rejects the declension model which is often associated by those who support it with New England's economic prosperity. Declension historians, then, see the increasing wealth, trade, and growth of the colony in terms of worldly concerns overtaking the spiritual. Taylor disagrees, stating, "The increasing commercialism of New England life at the end of the seventeenth century derive from Puritan values rather than manifested their decay."[123] For Taylor, a proper understanding of Puritan purposes includes a string commitment to work and prosperity as essential to "the Puritan's effort to glorify God."[124]

Cotton Mather observed that the church of the 1690s was dominated not by the John Winthrops, but by women: "There are far more godly Women in the World than there are Godly Men...I have seen it without going a Mile from home, That in a Church of between Three and Four Hundred Communicants, there are but few more than One Hundred Men; all the Rest are Women."[125] Women were influential in both church and community. Unlike the Chesapeake colonies, where the ratio of women to men was imbalanced, Massachusetts Bay settlers had come to the New World with wives and families. These families, formed communities, and wives lived and worked in social networks, not in isolation. As a result, women knew one another and talked often, sharing their opinions of the male leaders in the community. A man's reputation, in fact, was often made or broken by the community of females, a factor which Alan Taylor refers to as "oral power,"[126] so strong women were "frequently" taken to court to face charges of slander brought by men who feared the women's effect on their reputations.

Rather than too much economic growth, a disinterest on the part of males in the colony, or even doctrinal drift, many historians would place the blame for the colony's decline on the changing political situation in England. The continual struggle for the English monarch to assert absolute authority would make one last attempt when James II came to the throne after the death of the more lenient Charles II, the Restoration's king. James II's attempts at authority and "The crown's assumption of control over New England in 1684 effectively shattered 'any lingering sense among the colonists that they formed a special, divinely chosen community'". King James II, eager to assert his control over the New World, formed the Dominion of New England after revoking the Massachusetts Charter.

---

[122] James Nuechterlein, "The Myth of Declension." *First Things*, May 1, 1999.
[123] Taylor, 159.
[124] Taylor, 159.
[125] Taylor, 174.
[126] Ibid.

James II

By 1688, England had a Constitutional Monarchy ruled by monarchs who would share power with parliament and respect the individual rights and liberties that would appear in the English Bill of Rights a year later. The colony of Massachusetts would undergo further organizational changes and would come to play the greatest role in asserting its independence from Britain and sparking a revolution for independence. The fierce independence, strong work ethic, and refusal to conform that could be seen in many of Boston's outspoken citizens is surely the legacy of the Massachusetts Bay Colony that had long ceased to exist.

Online Resources

Other colonial America titles by Charles River Editors

Other titles about the Massachusetts Bay Colony on Amazon

Bibliography

Bremer, Francis J. John Winthrop: America's Forgotten Founding Father. New York: Oxford University Press, 2003.

Cave, Alfred A. The Pequot War. Amherst, MA: University of Massachusetts Press, 1996.

Clap, Roger. "Surviving the First Year of the Massachusetts Bay Colony, 1630-1631". National Humanities Center Resource Toolbox.

Crilly, Mark W. "John Winthrop: Magistrate, Minister, Merchant," The Midwest Quarterly 40, no. 2, 1999.

Dickinson, John. "Chapter V: The Massachusetts Charter and the Bay Colony (1628-1660)," in Commonwealth History of Massachusetts, ed. Albert Bushnell Hart, vol. 1. New York: States History Company, 1927.

Dillon, Francis. The Pilgrims: Their Journeys and Their World. New York: Doubleday and Company, 1975.

Emily Easton, Roger Williams: Prophet and Pioneer. Boston: Houghton, Mifflin, 1930.

Ellis, George E. The Puritan Age and Rule in the Colony of the Massachusetts Bay, 1629-1685. Boston: Houghton Mifflin. 1888.

Ernst, James. Roger Williams: New England Firebrand. New York: Macmillan, 1932.

Goodman, Nan. "Banishment, Jurisdiction, and Identity in Seventeenth-Century New England: The Case of Roger Williams," Early American Studies 7, no. 1, 2009.

Greene, Jack P. Pursuits of Happiness: The Social Development of Early Modern British Colonies and the Formation of American Culture. Chapel Hill, NC: University of North Carolina Press, 1988.

Morgan, Ted. Wilderness at Dawn: The Settling of the North American Continent. New York: Simon and Schuster, 1993.

Nuechterlein, James. "The Myth of Declension." First Things, May 1, 1999.

Philbrick, Nathaniel. Mayflower: A Story of Courage, Community, and War. New York: Viking, 2006.

Pratt, Casey. "Roger Williams's Unintentional Contribution to the Creation of American Capitalism," Libertarian Papers 3, 2011.

Richter, Daniel. Facing East from the Indian Country: A Native History of Early America. Cambridge: Harvard University Press. 2001.

Rugg, Winifred King. Unafraid: A Life of Anne Hutchinson. Boston: Houghton Mifflin, 1930.

Smith, Cheryl C. "Out of Her Place: Anne Hutchinson and the Dislocation of Power in New World Politics," Journal of American Culture. Malden, MA. 29, no. 4, 2006.

Taylor, Alan. American Colonies. New York: Viking, 2001.

Underhill, John. "The Pequot Wars". Connecticut History on the Web.

Vanburkleo, Sandra F. "To be rooted Out of Her Station: The Ordeal of Anne Hutchinson".

American Political Trials, ed. Michal R. Belknap. (Westport, CT: Praeger Publishers, 1994).

"We Shall Be as a City upon a Hill". Urban History Review 19, no. 1-2, 1990.

Winthrop, John. "A Model of Christian Charity." 1630. The Winthrop Society.

Made in the USA
San Bernardino, CA
02 March 2017